VISITING
INDIRA GANDHI'S
PALMIST

VISITING
INDIRA GANDHI'S
PALMIST

Kirun Kapur

KIRUN KAPUR

ELIXIR PRESS
DENVER, COLORADO

www.elixirpress.com

Book design by Steven Seighman
Author photo: J. Cash

Library of Congress Cataloging-in-Publication Data

Kapur, Kirun.
   [Poems. Selections]
   Visiting Indira Gandhi's Palmist / Kirun Kapur.
      pages ; cm.
   ISBN 1-932418-50-0 (alk. paper)
   I. Title.
   PS3611.A694A6 2014
   811'.6—dc23
                                    2013049683

ISBN-13: 9781932418521

10   9   8   7   6   5   4   3   2   1

For Mary Therese Breton and Inder Lal Kapur

CONTENTS

Acknowledgments   ix
Introduction   xi

Anthem   1

1.

Family Portrait, USA   5
Mango Is the King of Fruit   6
My Father's Hopscotch, 1942   8
He Who Does Not Have the Church As His Mother
    Does Not Have God As His Father   9
History (with a Melon Cleaver)   11
Meat and Marry   13
Dog, Master   14
First Families: Cain and Abel   15
Snakes   19
Poetry   20
Art History   22
Under the Bed   24
At the Convent of San Marco, Looking at Fra Angelico's
    Annunciation (or If Your Mother's Name Is Also Mary)   25
Polaroid City   27
Visiting Indira Gandhi's Palmist   29
The American, 1965   30
Nursery Rhymes (or The Time She Chased My Mother with
    a Carving Knife)   31
The Mango Tree in the Neighbor's Yard   33

2.

Light   37

Havan, 1921   39

Bollywood for Lovers   41

Chorus   43

I Ask My Father How It Happened   45

The History Family   46

Concerns   49

I Ask My Mother How It Happened   50

Dancing with My Father   51

3.

First Families: The Pandavas (and Assorted Princes)   57

4.

Basic Geography   71

First Families: Cain and Abel   74

My Brother's Keeper   79

Love Song (Orion's Belt: The King Brothers' Murder Trial,
       Florida, 2002)   81

Love Song (Surat, Gujarat, 1992)   83

At the Tiki Lounge   85

Nobody Nation   87

Fire, House, Me   92

You Give Me Fever   93

Arriving, New Delhi   94

From the Afterlife   95

For the Survivors   97

Notes   99

ACKNOWLEDGMENTS

Grateful acknowledgement is made to the editors of the following publications where these poems first appeared, sometimes in different forms:

AGNI: Part 2, section 1 of "First Families: Cain and Abel" (as "East")
AGNI ONLINE: "Anthem"
Arts & Letters: "Poetry," "You Give Me Fever," "From the Afterlife"
Atlanta Review: "The Mango Tree in the Neighbor's Yard"
Beloit Poetry Journal: "At the Tiki Lounge," "History (with a Melon Cleaver)" (as "Melon Cleaver"), "Light," Part 1, section 1 of "First Families: Cain and Abel" (as "Chapter and Verse")
Clapboard House: "Mango is the King of Fruit," "Meat and Marry," "Family Portrait, USA"
Cortland Review: "He Who Does Not Have the Church As His Mother Does Not Have God As His Father"
Crab Orchard Review: "Arriving, New Delhi," Part 2, section 2 of "First Families: Cain and Abel" (as "Prologue")
FIELD: "The American, 1965" (as "The American"), "Visiting Indira Gandhi's Palmist"
Fusion Magazine: "Dancing with My Father," "For the Survivors"
Mascara Review (AU): "My Father's Hopscotch, 1942," "Under the Bed"
Massachusetts Review: Part 2, section 3 of "First Families: Cain and Abel" (as "A Man From the Lord")
Michigan Quarterly Review: "At the Convent of San Marco, Looking at Fra Angelico's Annunciation..."
Poetry International: Part 1, section 3 of "First Families: Cain and Abel" (as "Chapter and Verse")
Seneca Review: "Havan, 1921"
Third Coast: "Love Song (Surat, Gujarat, 1992)"

"Mango is the King of Fruit," "Meat and Marry" and "Family Portrait, USA" appear in the anthology *Best of the House, 2013*.
"Poetry," "You Give Me Fever" and "From the Afterlife" were awarded the 2012 Arts & Letters/Rumi Prize for Poetry and were recorded for PRIME.

"Anthem" appears in Oxford University Press's anthology, *Identity: A Reader for Writers* and was featured in the Saturday Poetry Series.

I also wish to thank the following institutions (and the friends I found there) for their generosity: The Fine Arts Work Center in Provincetown, MacDowell Colony and The Vermont Studio Center. Some of these poems were written under their miraculous, congenial roofs.

For debts deep and various, I owe my gratitude to Letty and Jim Cash, Colrain, Carolina Ebeid and Jeff Pethybridge, Kevin Goodan, Kathy Graber (and VCFA friends), Carrie Green, Amalia Jiva, Mark Jones, Paul Kapur, Elizabeth Knapp, Laura Miller, Mio Osaki, Robert Pinsky, Rishi Reddi, Dawne Shand, Jake Strautmann and Rosanna Warren. My heart-felt thanks to Ned Balbo for selecting the book and to Dana Curtis for bringing it to life. For loving, reading and changing these poems (and me), endlessly and from the start, I thank Rachel DeWoskin and Fred Speers. For soul-saving company from the Arctic to the Empty Quarter, I thank Mark Vanhoenacker. For the generous, courageous, inspirational example of their lives, I thank my extraordinary parents, Inder and Terri Kapur. This book is for them.

Finally, and beyond measure, I am indebted to James Richard Cash and Silas Arjuna Cash—for making everything possible, for being plain joy.

INTRODUCTION

Kirun Kapur's debut volume *Visiting Indira Gandhi's Palmist* offers worlds of striking richness. From family lore marked by the 1947 partition of British India and the chaos that ensued, Kapur crafts a saga that is both personal and public. Her exploration of lives intersecting yet separated across time, culture, and continent reveals the many ways in which we carry, renounce, and rediscover the past. Kapur introduces us to an astonishing range of characters—a father who "speaks five languages, quotes Frost as easily as Ghalib" ("Meat and Marry"); a mother and onetime nun who foreswore her "Benedictine coif" for love ("Family Portrait, USA"); Cain and Abel of the Bible; Prince Arjuna of the Gita. At the heart of this quest, however, is an inquisitive mind examining our creation stories—personal, historical, and mythical. Through poems that are masterfully paced and densely layered, Kapur sets out to explore the tensions of our most basic human bonds: love and duty, violence and communion, family and nation.

Family stories define us; they offer myths of origin, a way to grasp our place in time. For Kapur, they are the raw material for more searching explorations than autobiography provides. A father's favorite fruit summons back the world he fled: "You can't go back," Kapur observes, "the skin un-split, the flesh intact, so you feed me/the King of Fruit; I eat till my stomach hurts" ("Mango Is the King of Fruit"). He is "The American, 1965" awed by the snow he's never seen: "So many flakes. So many falling toward him./They burn for a moment, white tongues." A mother, the former novice, explains desire through chocolate chip cookies—"*It's all our wanting that makes the world so sad*"— caught between past renunciations and the fulfillments of family life. Revisiting the past through art's transformative power, Kapur pays tribute to family's influence: she acknowledges all that's "added and taken from the sum of us," and observes with characteristic restraint, "It doesn't hurt//To be made of others' sadnesses" ("You Give Me Fever").

India's partition triggered one of history's great migrations, and Kapur captures its effects through the stories that survive. "Polaroid City" explores the father's escape from Rawalpindi via tonga—"A sort of poor man's taxi...a horse-drawn cart"—and train before mob violence and arson take hold of the city: "Picture apple blossoms for sale in the city,/Burnt limbs scattered across the springtime street." In this and other inventive pantoums, we encounter lives long past: "the blind man," a neighbor, "left dead on the porch, under a spotless sheet"; "Grandfathers, nieces, brothers, ashes of debate and rage"—all to prove "a fact of the family:/Even fate must be shared between us" ("The History Family"). The pantoum's repetitions are perfect for the poet's purpose: people and narratives recur, pulling the poem back on course, references reasserting themselves as if to keep from vanishing.

Elsewhere, personal history widens into myth, the founding stories of every culture in which family bonds come first. In "First Families: Cain and Abel," the archetypal narrative of sibling rivalry and envy casts light on the idea of tribe and nation. Here, Cain views his mother Eve as "rebel"—"she was irresistible to anyone with privilege"—and Adam as "authority" embodied: "My father learned and changed into what follows rebels./ Government, I mean, if you're lucky." But this balance is not sustained: "We became a family: what follows after/love, I mean, a partition." The dynamics that divide families divide nations as well, and Cain is caught up in larger forces, a darker fate: "It's not as though this were wholly my plan." From the politics of division to the bonds of blood, Kapur's quest narrows into a single question: "Does the candle in my hand burn with the same flame my father drew from that match? Or are they separate fires—" ("I Ask My Father How It Happened"). The answer is, it's both—a separate fire and one that's shared—her link to the past intact despite the need to break away.

Even more impressive is "First Families: The Pandavas (and Assorted Princes)," an ambitious retelling of the Gita in which Kapur alternates between mythic episodes of honor and fratricide (starting with Prince Arjuna "whose dread/of killing those he loved,/who had loved him, pressed pause// on the great battle of his brothers v. his cousins") and sections explicitly focused on Kapur's roots, braiding her narrative legacy with events from the Hindu epic so as to enrich their mutual resonance and depth. The lives that Kapur channels show great vividness and range:

Is this how our Prince transformed his heart?
How he cut and scattered all the strings
that tied him to the lives of brothers, mothers, sons

among the weeds and black earth churned
by angry hooves?

Myth and history hold great influence; they show us who we are through the mirror of the past. But even mirrors may deceive. Kapur, of course, is aware of this: she never loses sight of the line between fact and fiction, though its integrity isn't always absolute. Many of her poems derive from family and historical events (and gain greater resonance for doing so), but more important than literal truth is their aesthetic power and the poet's insights into darkness and desire. By selecting exactly the right material to convey in compelling language, she shapes a personal and family saga that is truly unforgettable, unadorned by needless ornament yet powerful and wide-ranging. In "From the Afterlife," Kapur explores her place: the poet now is history—all the people she's encountered in life or imagination—and art's great gift—to transcend a lifetime—is an offering of words:

…Turns out, I never was a girl, I was all

those girls, a girl statue, the torch raised, you know the one—
standing in the harbor, wearing a sari.

The tide foams up. Now, I'm so much dust,
I am a continent, absorbing—a thimble full

of mother, angry powder, laughing specks, froth,
filth, lover, crying cinders, particles of mineral wind.

I'm proof that nothing is lost.
You can breathe me in.

Such lines, beautifully crafted and pitch-perfect, offer poetry of the highest order, embodying the controlled, expressive syntax that is a hallmark of *Visiting Indira Gandhi's Palmist*. "After the riot of years," Kirun Kapur asks in "Light," "How should we remember the old stories?" The answer lies in these poems—passionate, connected by a wry sense of humor, wise to the archetypes that history celebrates or suppresses, and infused with a compassion attentive to our human story.

—Ned Balbo, November 2013

There are only two or three human stories, and they go on repeating themselves as fiercely as if they had never happened before; like the larks in this country, that have been singing the same five notes over for thousands of years.

—Willa Cather, *O Pioneers*

ANTHEM

Love begins in a country
Where oranges weep sweetness
And men piss in the street.

Your hands are forever binding
Black strands in a plait. Your mother's
Childhood friend has steeped

Your skin in coconut oil, tucked
Her daughter beside you—the night
Is a womb, live with twins.

Heat's body presses every body.
Sharp chop of your uncle's cough
Clocks the hours; your sister's washing,

The rush of your thoughts. Morning
Is nine glass bangles hoisting sacks
Of sugar from the floor. I'm not talking

About a place, but a country:
Its laws are your mother, its walls
Are your dreams. The flag it flies

Is your father, waving.

1.

FAMILY PORTRAIT, USA

One photograph—the only—with another woman's writing on the back:
New Mexico. Novitiate. 1963?

Nearly impossible to see my mother beneath the Benedictine coif—
Nineteen young nuns in a row, each face

Framed separately by immaculate white wimples.
This was my mother's family,

Between the family she left and the family she made—
Nineteen sisters carved like cameos, bright, but indistinct.

It was cold. We milked cows in a barn.
When we sang, "Cast away the dreams of darkness," I could see

Those words carried over the hay, on our breath.
At night, in the basement, nineteen women swabbed the backs of refugees.

I didn't know who they were. It didn't matter. An open sore
Is an open sore. You don't need to know anything about it.

I want to see, though I know my mother's face:
The French nose; the brown eyes greened in anger.

I have no faith, just a sore and a story. I want to come to a place
Where I don't need to know anything more about it.

MANGO IS THE KING OF FRUIT
for my father

The T.V. entertains itself. My eyes
on you, spattering the tabletop with pulp,
the orange fruit, the knife

of equal brightness. The story goes:
your brother stole the fruit,
his khaki shorts lost up the trunk,

then shoes hung down, twin crows.
You played look-out: cane field up the road,
kept your school-shirt clean, stopped passers-by

with made-up Shakespeare, breaking news
of Gandhi-ji, until the coast was clear.
The owner never caught you,

though he chased with rocks and threats
of the police. Your brother ran ahead,
while you tossed back, *Sir—Uncle—*

No need to be mad, even Lord Ganesh ran
a race to win a mango. And he was also fat!
Uncle-ji— don't run so fast. Your face

is getting redder than the butt of a baboon...
You feed me straight from your hand,
saying *Sorry, it's not an Indian*

mango. From Mexico, I think. Now, your brother's
five years dead. Your good arm shakes.
The juice has stamped a yellow hemisphere

into the placket of your shirt. You can't go back,
the skin un-split, the flesh intact, so you feed me
the King of Fruit; I eat until my stomach hurts.

We turn to watch a cartoon cat with an axe
pursue a brown mouse over a ledge.
Underneath, there waits a pack of patient dogs.

We laugh, mop up. *Run*—you warn
both mouse and cat—*run faster, brothers.*

My Father's Hopscotch, 1942

Five rooftops—wide and flat— lie shining
between his father's and his uncle's house.
Five rivers in Punjab. His path spools out,
a conqueror, marching through the Khyber Pass.

First jump: Auntie Shara's wicked chilies
smirking in the sun. Second: Rana Bhai's old goat,
who gives no milk and bites a younger brother's ass.
On Naana's roof, a locked-up room, a sharp-nosed girl

whose only word is *snakes*. At his command:
a village burns, troops swim the Jhelum in the night.
Midway, my father stops, salaams
the black-draped Begums who come up to take the air.

They praise him as their *naughty one,* feed him
chunks of jaggery, never exposing their hands.
Who are you today, little son? Alexander? Shah Jahan?
Don't tell us you're an Englishman!

The infantry is restless. Rumors in the street.
Some rumbling, a mutiny: the East is lost,
turn back, return to Greece. Roof to roof,
he leaps, he presses on across the map.

He Who Does Not Have The Church As His Mother Does Not Have God As His Father

My mother was the sort of daughter
who knew the doctor's number;
whether the spoons were polished;

which hand-cut glasses, sparkling
in her mother's dark china cabinet
hid vodka or gin. She knew

the exact number of steps between
her bed and the landing, the landing
and the front door; whether there was milk

or ice or aspirin; when to spend
two nights with neighbors, quietly
washing their dishes. She read

to be certain when Lily of The Valley
would bloom, under downstairs windows,
near her father, entombed in his chair.

A crucifix swung from her bedroom wall,
the sober Mary hung in the hall, patiently
steadying her baby. My mother

buttoned her own coat to the chin,
repeated *The Lord's Prayer*,
so she wouldn't waste time

on talk about the handsome French dentist,
his poor child and that Irish wife.
When she found four children

alone in the woods, she knew
exactly what to do: she towed them home
and washed them in her mother's perfumed oil.

HISTORY (WITH A MELON CLEAVER)

The summer of 1947 was not like other Indian summers.
Even the weather had a different feel…When the creation of
the new state of Pakistan was formally announced, ten million
people—Muslims, Hindus and Sikhs—were in flight. By the
time the monsoon broke, almost a million of them were dead,
and all of northern India was in arms, in terror or in hiding.

—Kushwant Singh, *Train to Pakistan*

They stood in line to buy a slice of melon—
My father and my uncle, in cantaloupe season.
When the boy in front reached out to pay,
The melon seller waved his cleaver.

This was Lahore in cantaloupe season:
Summer was working up its heat.
With one hand the melon seller waved his cleaver
Over a bright, thick slab of fruit.

Summer was only beginning,
But already the days had grown hot.
A cool slab of sweet melon
Was everything two boys could want.

But already the days had grown heated
When the boy in front reached out to pay.
Chilled melon was all two boys could want,
Or so my uncle claimed.

When the boy reached out to pay,
The melon seller brandished his cleaver.
My uncle paused before claiming,
With the other hand, he stabbed the boy with a dagger.
The melon seller brandished his cleaver,

Drawing all eyes from the fruit.
He stabbed the boy with a tiny dagger,
Putting his other hand to use.

All eyes flew to the cleaver—
The boy fell on our feet.
No one was watching the other hand.
This is how my uncle told it.

The boy fell on our feet.
My uncle's voice was full of wonder.
This is the way he told it—
As if a comet had passed overhead.

My uncle's voice was full of wonder:
The boy was reaching out to pay.
As if a comet had passed over
My father and uncle in melon season.

Meat and Marry

A nun and a swami walk into a bar. O.K., not a bar, exactly—unless you count the salad bar—but, she is a nun and in the cafeteria of International House she walks in on her life, part joy, part joke. The room bustles—Asians, Africans, Scandinavians—a UN with plastic knives. It's 1965. She's spent several years in a convent, so even white Americans look stunningly foreign. A guide is talking, rearranging the pleats of a peacock silk sari. My mother tries to focus on her voice—high, tipping suddenly, like a flute played on a roller coaster: *no pork at this table, here no beef, Kosher, chopsticks, here no meat.* She can't identify the food. Nine kinds of turban are within reach. People course by—black, blonde, red, yellow—they carry flimsy trays, but speak so earnestly. Out of this Technicolor glory, the world's every possible character—my father. Out of the whole universe of words, he'll speak just one, in English. He is the same hue as her first, brown leather Bible; his eyes flash like the buckles on a young nun's shoe. She'll learn he isn't a swami, he speaks five languages, quotes Frost as easily as Ghalib. She turns in a confused circle. He doesn't touch her, just inclines his head politely toward his own plate. His voice is low, like a rocking boat, *Eat.*

DOG, MASTER

It's a game. My brother
standing on our parents' bed and me,
the knees and elbows next to him.

His job to order me to sit or roll,
then hit me with a pillow, training Doggie.
My job to disobey, then take him out

below the knees, with growling.
My mother in the doorway,
her face slack with dismay, sees

our instinct clearly, to love each other
viciously, right over the end
of the bed. Fierce arguments:

the Doggie cannot leave her knees;
the Master cannot bend. The play is equal
parts brute strength and lawyering.

Each dog knows home and every master
owns the music that will put the beast to sleep.
Whatever beats in us, beat and played

this way once. I remember
looking up—his one arm raised,
his face wracked with laughter.

First Families: Cain and Abel

1. Cain

Now the man knew his wife Eve. Only fools call me
a rebel. The rebel was my mother. Like every rebel

she was irresistible to anyone with privilege
and without authority. She only half knew what she was doing,

but she knew she was right. She loved right
more than she loved my father.

How could he help but want her and the fruit?
How could he help but hate her. Garden verse

is the complaint of lovers who wished to be loved better.
And she conceived and bore Cain and said

I have gotten a man from the Lord. Next she bore his brother.
But here the words just leap ahead without the story.

My father learned and changed into what follows rebels.
Government, I mean, if you're lucky.

We became a family: what follows after love,
I mean, a partition.

2. Abel

Everyone asks why
he did it or worse yet
why the Father, knowing it all
in advance, allowed my life
to rain on the asparagus. I ask
why didn't I kill him first?
What would I have done were I the one
who survived? All those times
I wrestled him to the edge
of the bluff, held his face
under the green water
of the irrigation ditch, I could have
played the part of the mysterious
first villain. I still dream
of the deep bass sound
my shepherd's staff made
when my aim was good and it met
the sweet melon of his head.
It was the first warm day in June.

3. Cain

Now Abel was keeper
of sheep, and Cain
a tiller of the ground.

And from that sentence my own began.

Who teaches
a boy to keep
sheep or a man to plow?

It's not as though this were wholly my plan.

But when I saw

the girlish legs of early carrots,
the bent wheat shake
its head as it lunged upright again,

when my mother ran out with her feet still bare
in search of the first
purple irises, then

I became guilty of anything.

In the course of time
Cain brought to the Lord
an offering of the fruit of the ground

And Abel brought
the firstlings
of his flock, their fat portions.

I remember

every bulb and shoot.
A garland of last year's
onion; barley, spelt.

And the Lord had
regard for Abel and his offering,
but for Cain he had no

regard. Garlic
in a braid; two fists of dill,
the fronds like feathers.

So Cain was very angry and his countenance fell.
The Lord said to Cain,
"Why are you angry?"

Pomegranates, quince; rocket, celery root!

I was arguing
for dahlias and sorrel,
lemons on their squat, blunt trees.

It was the first I knew of who I was.

SNAKES

He said, *You will not do it,* and he wouldn't
look me in the face. I watched him
pace between the window and the bed
until he turned away completely,
his hand still against the pane.
I felt the thudding in my chest
like eels smacking their heads
in the stew pot before the lid is sealed.
He said, again, *You will not do it.*
So I raised the cut snake
of my braid a little higher, unable
to say, *Papa, I already did.*

POETRY

Truth is, I loved to anger him
    Sometimes, loved for us both
    To feel too much for speech.

He never had to shout—
    Not under my roof!
    Because I said so—

Though my crimes were many:
    Misused newspapers from Islamabad
    (He'd waited 15 weeks to hold)

To make a papier-mâché penis,
    For science class, of course; refused
    To wear a proper dress; for guests,

Recited limericks I'd learned from Timmy Prinze.
    He quoted Hafiz—
    His Persian arced above my head,

A shock of glittery finches arguing—
    Or Mir, whose Urdu was a scatter shot
    Of words I knew and words I didn't:

Pop pop pop,
    They struck me like the heels
    Tooled by the roadside cobbler

Who chatted while he hammered nails into my soles.
    I thought I understood
    The message: I was too ignorant

To grasp the depth of chastisement I'd earned,
    Too ignorant to warrant further talk.
    Now, I read those poems for myself,

Those moments we were wholly foreign to
    Each other, that defied
    Their plain translated meaning,

But linked vowel to gaping vowel,
    Crashing rhyme to rhyme—
    His furious mouth controlled by meter.

He said enough to strike me dumb, to make me
    Struggle for some sense. He was arming me
    With shoes to wear, with fury, feathers, flight.

ART HISTORY

Leviticus 19:34: But the stranger that dwelleth with you...thou
shalt love him as thyself.

I'd even smoke the angels,
that's what he liked to say,
checking his face in the mirror, shining
up his gun. *He isn't well,* his wife
explained, on the strip of grass
our houses faced. I watched the tremor
in her lip, her fingers uncurling from fists.

Hey, Rosy Girl, he'd call, when I passed by.
Hey, Nipples. I stood still
while my mouth gaped on
those golden words
I'd seen fly from the face
of every angel, delivering God's news.

He stood with the garage door up.
Two chairs. The toolbox, where he kept
the gun, served as a table top. *My home
away from home.* He laughed,
came toward me with a wad of ones,
*For beer and smokes. Go down the block,
unless you want to come on in. Miss Nipples.*
I realized he was handsome, then
felt air burn in my chest.

Later, in a hotel bed, I watched the burning
tip of my lit cigarette and thought of him.
I'd learned the faces of the angels, painted
into walls. Their mouths, their errands,
how each mission ends: a heap of salt,
a hat of thorns, pure spirit with no body—
not women and not men. I'd heard
he burned the house down, smoking
in his bed. His wife had left
and I'd, of course, moved on by then.

UNDER THE BED

I didn't need monsters, I had
history. Didn't want history,
I wanted crime—though I had

a girl's body and the wind
in the palms outside cried steadily,
sounding like rain. I didn't need

heaven or sin or punishment.
I had a mother. I had a father.
A fine gold sand blew across my face

and the shoreline I stood on changed.
The god of our house ruled
patiently. The gods of my heart

devoured me. I didn't need a heart,
I had a family. A sea
pumped that vast salt-love

through its chambers.
When I looked under the bed,
I discovered emptiness.

Discovering my emptiness, I sang.

At the Convent of San Marco, Looking at Fra Angelico's *Annunciation* (or If Your Mother's Name Is Also Mary)

Into the fresco's sunlit room, the word
falls, a stone that she can't move. She knows

the tomb is sealed and sees the end illuminated.
Her miracle takes seconds. Shocked

to find the day resumed, she stumbles with the news—
she will live. I'm studying

the light, the faint cracks in the paint,
the mother, handmaid, wife:

the moment she is nailed to it.
My mother was born in broad day,

roof of her mouth un-fused and christened, Mary.
Father O'Grady held the babe, urged surgery:

Without the ability to properly confess her sins,
the mouth of Hell awaits her. I wait

for Mary to speak in the convent's cell,
walls scrubbed white—the Angel's perfect face

already turning away—wondering if a soul hangs
on what can be spoken clearly. My mother was one

of many: Mary Therese, Mary Margaret,
Mary Benedicta, Mary Genevieve, Mary

of the cleft palate and the ether mask,
who must be careful not to whistle when she speaks,

Mary, painted as though it happened right
where I stand, under a monk's peaked doorway,

that she bent half over her book and spoke.
I'll tell you this, in the worst minute

of my life, I didn't recognize my feet or hands,
too bright, too hard to breathe, but I could hear

a voice instructing me: *Put on your shoes.*
Put on your shoes and stand.

POLAROID CITY

We took a tonga to the train station,
That's all my father says.
Away at school in 1947, reading
A Tale of Two Cities, in Rawalpindi.

Here's what my father says:
A tonga is a horse and cart.
London! Paris! from his room in Pindi—
He read faster. What would happen next?

A sort of poor man's taxi, a tonga is a horse-drawn cart.
One animal hauling the weight of others—
He had no idea what was coming next.
He wrote to his brothers, *I study Urdu, English, Hindi.*

One animal dragging others—
That was spring in Rawalpindi.
In Punjabi, he wrote to his brothers,
There's a new kind of camera in New York City!

It was a beautiful spring in Rawalpindi
When a Muslim dhobi warned his hostel full of Hindu boys.
While his eye flashed like a camera on the city,
My father escaped before the mob arrived.

When a Muslim dhobi saved his hostel full of Hindu boys,
March flowers were for sale in the city.
Three boys escaped in a tonga, before the school flashed up in flames.
My father always asks me, *What is the dhobi's English name?*

Picture apple blossoms for sale in the city,
Burnt limbs scattered across the springtime street.
Do you know what a dhobi is? he always asks me.
A dhobi is a washer-man. He beats your clothes clean with a stick.

Brown arms, trim brown branches in the springtime street:
We took a tonga to the train station—
We took a tonga to the train station —
It's all my father can say.

Visiting Indira Gandhi's Palmist

I don't know when I realized he had one eye that watched me, alive, the other free to read the heavens. Could he see I grew where others couldn't? Could he read my face, in its lines all their faces—my aunt's that morning, in the mirror beside mine, hissed, *don't stare, don't forget details, it's your honor to look for all of us.* Did he see I hated his eye, sometimes, hated my honor: the hand always above me. Which eye reads that hand? Which eye can judge its weight? I wanted to look away. Wanted to cry. His untethered eye was milky as a teacup. *Why have you come here, daughter?* Couldn't say, *My father made me.* Couldn't blame, *You looked at Her hand, but you didn't save Her from a firing squad.* I wouldn't confess, *I am afraid I'll spend my life under a hand that I can't stop or hold.* He never touched my palm, imbedded with pencil lead, or the moon under my thumb, scarred while opening a can. He assured me I'd make a fine wife, a fine mother of fine sons, prove to be a credit to my family, while his iris swiveled like a wobbly fan. I made up my mind right then to open my hands—their forked wires, their lines of names and places—take them.

THE AMERICAN, 1965

On 133rd—between the Mormon boys
And the shawarma shop—the sky opens

And sends flakes falling from a wide darkness.
My father's 40 years unravel:

Hail over green sugar cane;
A rose-red wedding sari, deliberately unwound;

Carved into mountain walls, the basalt lips of God;
A neighbor, hanging by his turban

From a flowering black plum tree;
The 25th day of monsoon rain;

Ladies shoes, shot out the window of a train;
The highest peak in the measured world;

Twice, the shuddering of a brand new flag.
None of this lessens his shock—

So many flakes. So many falling toward him.
They burn for a moment, white tongues.

Nursery Rhymes
(or The Time She Chased My Mother
with a Carving Knife)

All around the cobbler's bench,
you, Mother, who were taught
to overlook the stench of last night's gin,
to kneel, say prayers over all your sins,

but the glint of the knife was louder
than anything Mother Superior,
Mother Goose said, louder than crinoline
and rings and the ticking of heels on linoleum,

Jack be nimble Jack be quick, don't be afraid
you'll slip, fear eats up time, eats candle sticks,
the chime of your childhood will find its silence,
quietly untie, like a shoelace—Oh, Mother, may I

stand between you and my grandmother,
you and you not being my mother, I believe
it was the holy ghost of me, there in the foyer,
dining room, kitchen, in the living room blocking

her drunken way, keeping her from falling
on the knife, keeping you 20 paces ahead
whispering, *hush little baby don't say a word*,
someday you will buy me a mocking bird,

which will turn out to be a parakeet I name Anela,
Hawaiian for angel, but first we must go
all around the mulberry bush, mulberry bush,
mulberry bush, it was too early for me

and you still had to be the daughter, but I was
the spirit pushing the closet door shut, begging,
stay hidden a while longer, then open the door to me,
I'm coming to you angry and blind as mice.

THE MANGO TREE IN THE NEIGHBOR'S YARD

All my choices have not been choices
    A good daughter makes.

And the pit is the shape of my eye, seeing
    Being the hard center of life. Don't cry

For what you can't reach;
    All fruit falls eventually—

That's what I learned by watching
    The tree. And when no one was watching

Me, I waded into the sweet
    Reek and bees, stepping

Around split gold hemispheres, smashed seeds—
    Ready to take the hurt world into me.

2.

The suffering and grief of Partition are not memorialized at the border, nor publically, elsewhere, in India, Pakistan and Bangladesh. Millions may have died, but they have no monument. Stories are all that people have, stories that rarely breach the frontiers of family and religious community: people talking to their own blood.

—Urvashi Butalia, *The Other Side of Silence*

Only a few, survivors, bloom again in the rose, the tulip.
Think of all those faces, gone down under the dust.

—Mirza Asadullah Khan Ghalib

LIGHT

The only aunt I know would tell me,
This is how you knead the dough.
I don't remember the old stories—
Make sure it doesn't get too tough!

Knead carefully to make the atta.
Good girls know how to make good puris.
Make sure the gluten doesn't toughen,
A puri should be light and golden.

Good girls know how to make good puris.
They don't ask for the old stories.
A puri should be light and golden,
Like your cousin's and your cousin's cousin's.

I overheard the stories
When all the women shared a bed.
My cousins and my cousin's cousins—
The older women slept still dressed in saris.

When all the women shared a bed
The fan chuffed through a cloud of talcum powder.
Still fully dressed in saris,
They whispered names I'd never heard before.

When the fan chuffed sandalwood and roses,
I raised my arm above my head.
They named lost aunts and daughters.
I caught hold of my cousin's hand.

I raised my arm up in the dark.
There was a niece who could have been recovered.
I held my favorite cousin's hand.
Her name meant *light*, like mine does.

There was one niece who could have been recovered.
My grandfather had her traced.
Her name meant *light*, as mine does.
I've tried not to imagine her face.

Somehow my grandfather found her,
But her brothers refused to take her back.
I imagine the row of our faces,
Women in bed in the dark.

Her brothers refused to reclaim her.
This was after the riots and trains.
In bed, in the dark they could say it:
This is what broke us apart.

After the riot of years,
How should we remember the old stories?
What will break and what will toughen—
The only aunt I know will tell me.

HAVAN, 1921

It is my claim that as soon as we have completed the boycott of foreign cloth we shall have evolved so far that we shall necessarily give up the present absurdities and remodel national life in keeping with the ideal of simplicity and domesticity implanted in the bosom of the masses.

—Mohandas K. Gandhi

He struck a match and put it to the pile,
poured kerosene from buckets on the reams
of saffron, ruby, indigo silk finished
in an eighteen carat thread, milk-white voile
edged with tiny vines of ivy. He must

have trailed his wife all day, directing her
to gather every stitch of cloth that came
from mills in England—napkins, curtains,
petticoats—while he lectured about economies;
first patiently explaining loss and gain
then shouting: *They take lymph out of an Indian*
vein, pay Englishmen an English wage
to fix it up some way, then sell it to the arm
they drained for fifty rupees and a paisa.

The beds were stripped. The towels
rounded up. Placemats, woolens, handkerchiefs,
a drawer of favorite saris offered to the flames
of an idea taking hold; a blaze
that crinkled linen, muslin, into ash.

Who watched my father's father swing
the empty pail, his mother laugh, knowing
what the town would say? If they had known
how far that fire would spread—Delhi, Lahore,
the trains, sisters, daughters—would it have changed
the hopes fed to the pyre? And what of Mr. Spires,

Englishman and tutor to my uncles?
Was he thinking of the end of empires
that day, pausing his cycle in the lane
before the house, sweating, swatting
the flies away? He must have tugged the collar
of his broadcloth suit and wondered
at the line of smoke that pointed straight
into the lair of every country's gods—
a dark finger on a hand of brilliant prayers.

BOLLYWOOD FOR LOVERS

My father was in love with *Ratan*,
Movie lyrics written by his mother's cousin from Lahore:
Your glance has lit my heart on fire...
Hearts glittered on the screen in 1944.

With lyrics by his mother's cousin,
My father disappeared into the dark.
Hearts glittered on the screen in 1947:
You can't just leave. I'll stop you. I'll cover your feet with my tears.

My father disappeared into the dark—
Those movies ran for hours and hours.
You can't leave lovers, their fires and tears.
Outside, Lahore burned brightly, the jewel of cities.

Those movies often ran for hours.
The songs were everybody's favorite part.
Lahore flashed brightly as the jewel of cities:
Gardens, dancing girls and the British High Court.

Songs are the movie's heartbeat.
My father listened in the dark.
A good lyricist must write for every plot—
Even dead bodies blocking the door.

My father sat listening in the dark
When riots began in Lahore.
When bodies stacked up in the doorway,
His eyes remained locked on the screen.

When the riots began in Lahore,
The hero and heroine were dancing without touching.
His eyes remained locked on the brightness—
He watched the lovers cry and burn.

The hero and heroine danced without touching:
One glance is all it takes to light the spark…
For hours, he could not look away
Love spinning and burning, filling up the dark.

One glance is all it takes to light the spark…
The city ignited. The city cried and raged.
Love spinning and burning, filling up the dark—
Once you've seen it, you can never look away.

He walked home while the city ignited:
Gardens, girls, the old high court,
Once you've seen it, you can never look away—
A scene that keeps turning, a movie that plays and plays.

Later, my father wrote his own songs for the movies.
Bollywood was booming, the world had changed.
Some movies play on forever—
"Movie" is American, my father gently reproves me.

Bollywood is booming and the world has changed.
Now, my father never likes the movies.
We called them films, the cinema, he reminds me.
A good lyricist could lighten up the darkest plot.

Now, my father rarely likes a movie,
Though once he sat through *Ratan* in the dark.
A good lyricist can lighten any darkness,
Or so my father thought in 1944.

Chorus

He was my mother's sister's cousin's boy.
    A train streaked red, like on a holiday.

In the papers, they say it was a mob. Mobs. A whole village
    west of Civil Lines. We heard

that soldiers would be deployed. We heard
    you couldn't drink anymore from the Ravi.

We called her Pinky, though her name was Parvati.
    As she died, she told me,

inside her skull she could see the sky.
    What is the point in crying?

Mala, Tara, Devi, Rani. Reports
    may be exaggerated. I stopped believing my eyes.

Hindus halting northbound trains.
    Muslims stopping southbound trains.

Hot oil. Machetes. I watched with my own eye.
    Did I tell you, we called her Twinkle,

though her name was Aysha? I don't know how to explain.
    All the women's breasts cut off.

I believe some reports were exaggerated.
    Samir, Sadiq, Saleem, Sonny.

I couldn't say how many.
    We planted wheat those days. We planted melon.

As he lit the match he whispered,
    My son, you must cover your eyes.

We were a village of 15 men.
    We were 25 hiding in the donkey's shed.

I would have killed them, gladly
    but they were already dead.

Veena, Sita, Zara, Asha. Don't. Please don't—
    She traded her life for mine.

2 million. 12.5 million. 22 million. On foot.
    By air. By bullock cart. Vanished. No trace.

We left everyone behind. The man who carried her away,
    I'd known him my whole life.

The milkman I called Uncle.
    The neighbor I called Brother. The woman down the road

we all called Sister. Dragged by her hair. Found in a well.
    Her name was Mumtaz, but we called her Little One.

His name was Rafiq; his name was Ram Das.
    Someone you've known. Someone you saw

with your own eye. I don't talk about it.
    The bedroom ankle deep in silk and kerosene.

I Ask My Father How It Happened

Match flame burning toward his fingertip, my father lights a single candle: *This is how it is explained in old books. Slokas, sutras, stories, you know—* I watch him wave the match out as he hands me one lit taper from a set of ten. I light the second from the first. *Again,* he says. *Again.* Until he has to get another box. Here's the riddle of the past: Does the candle in my hand burn with the same flame my father drew from the match? Or are they separate fires—the one that fights the wax different from the one that stutters and burns fastest in the draft? He puts his hand on my head. I can't stop trying—again, again—until his voice cuts through and I notice, all our walls are stained with light.

The History Family

They left by train,
One bullet-proof vest between them.
My grandfather and his brother raged,
We can't leave! How can we stay?

One bullet-proof vest; eight people.
There are limits to what you can share.
How do you know what's worth leaving?
The brothers debated and raged.

In a family you have to share everything,
I can hear my father explain:
Whatever may rage between brothers,
A family shares what it has.

I can hear my father explaining,
When a cousin loved my bright red bangle:
A family shares what it has—
You must take it off and give it to her.

When a cousin loved my favorite bangle,
A mysterious fact was explained.
I took it off and I gave it—
It was lovelier on her wrist than on mine.

This is a fact of the family:
Even fate must be shared between us.
My grandfather wanted to leave,
But he agreed to wait and see.

He wanted the family to leave;
His brother thought it would all blow over.
How much are you prepared to see?
Whose fate are you willing to share?

His brother was sure it would all blow over.
Their neighbors had been neighbors for generations.
They had a long shared history:
A cup of sugar, an extra rupee, advice about the weather.

The neighbors had always been neighbors
And now they'd become something else.
Scrounging up extra rupees,
My grandfather bought the vest.

No one can guess what will change them.
One day a blind man was found dead;
My grandfather finished with waiting—
He knew who would go, who'd be left.

The blind man had lived one street over,
Left dead, on the porch, under a spotless sheet.
One brother would go and one would stay.
Their fates split between them so cleanly.

He left them behind on the porch,
His brother, his nieces, his nephews.
Their shared fate shattered between them:
A family is just you and a mirror.

My grandfather's eight went to India,
Were there when Independence was proclaimed.
A family is a house full of mirrors.
I've never asked, *Who wore the vest?*

My father was there on Independence Day—
Freedom flags, banners, fireworks and a long parade.
The vest was saved for another day, for the family
In the mirror, that would never leave by train.

CONCERNS

(after Andrew Motion)

This is a poem about games.
The four children laid out neatly
under a Jacaranda tree are playing.
When the summer twilight
thickens, when orange petals drop
over their eyes, it foretells
nothing. See the sturdy bodies
rise from their leaf-beds. See
that when three chase one
it is with the joy of having horses
gallop in their chests. When a bird
of prey passes overhead, tipping
its wings in the thermals, when
an engine backfires in the far-off haze,
nothing will happen. No one will die.
This poem is about games. One child
pressing her face to the gruff bark,
the others scattering in puffs
like the dry dust under their quick
stomping feet. Someone is counting,
someone is searching and calling
out names. Someone's passing
has caused tiny yellow roses to shake.
Don't be concerned. This is about nothing,
just games. You don't have to worry.
You don't have to be afraid.

I Ask My Mother How It Happened

It's noon. She takes the blue box from the pantry shelf and sits a cookie on the table. Chips Ahoy. Brown circle decked with darker flecks of brown. I can smell the chocolate, imagine the taste, while outside black and yellow mynas fight in the plumeria tree. *Do you want it? Would you like a taste?* I'm about to reach for it when she smiles, studying me: *That's how it happens.* The sun pours in, the birds are taking their grievances from tree to tree and the sweet, dark smell intensifies. Her eyes are chocolaty, so I know it's safe to ask, *Because of cookies?* She laughs and what I want more than the whole box is to make her do it again. *Because of desire. It's all our wanting that makes the world so sad.* I rub my sandals on the chair leg, fidget in my seat. This seems important. I'm thinking Chips Ahoy taste too dry, anyway. She stands, moving to put the box away. *In the convent, we prayed that Christ would live in our hearts, driving all other desires away.* I study the arch of her narrow back as she tidies the cupboard. She's wearing a green dress that I know she doesn't like. *It's only a cookie,* I say, but I know how I'd feel if someone took what I want most away. *It's o.k. You can eat it,* she says. The lesson is over. The birds have gone. Only the sun is left slicing the room with its clean, bright sword. *Eat it,* she urges, but even hours later, when I creep downstairs to say goodnight, the sweetness sits untouched on the empty tabletop.

DANCING WITH MY FATHER

If you could go back in time,
do you think you could have saved them?

> Time is an illusion, you know
> that.

But if you could go back—
explain, persuade them. Convince
even one uncle or niece. One stranger.

> The whole world is maya,
> illusion and dance.

Well, if you could stop the illusion.

> The Upanishads say…

I don't care what the *Upanishads* say.
What do you say? If you could go back,
if you could stop the illusion that was their death.

> I don't know who raised you
> to be so crude.

Surely, my crudeness is an illusion.

> You should eat more loki; it's good
> for you. It's made with plenty of haldi. You
> know, they are doing studies at Harvard
> about haldi.

Did you ever wish you'd died instead?

No, here's what I want to ask:
Have you felt angry for surviving?
All this time, is that how you've felt?

                                        You should eat.

Dad.

                                    They say it stops Alzheimer's.

                                Didn't I send you to good schools?

                                Didn't they teach you to ask smarter
                                                            questions?

                                                        It's a dance.

That's not an answer.

                                            Even now we are dancing.

I don't want to dance.

                                    Many steps and many gestures.

I don't want squash. Or turmeric. I hate loki.

> It has a beautiful flower. Can you
> hate a flower?

I *can* hate a flower. I've always hated loki.

> And a dance? Who can hate the twirl
> and the leap; the drums and the bells?

3.

Dhrita-Rashtra: On the field of Truth, on the battlefield of life, what came to pass, when my sons and their warriors faced those of my brother, the Pandavas?

—*The Bhagavad Gita,* verse 1

First Families: The Pandavas (and Assorted Princes)

Arjuna saw them standing there:
fathers, grandfathers, teachers,
uncles, brothers, sons,
grandsons and friends...

wanting war

That Prince of Princes,
Arjuna, whose dread
of killing those he loved,
who had loved him, pressed pause

on the great battle
of his brothers v. his cousins

for just a moment,

his chariot pacing between the armies of his world.

If he refused to fight, his brothers
would be slaughtered and their kingdom lost.

And if he fought, then he would kill
the cousins who had been like brothers.

And either way the field would fill
with ends of men all shouting,

Arjuna.

There—

time rolled and rolled out endlessly.

He waited.

And when he plunged
back in the fray of brothers, it was
the blue-skinned, milk-maid-loving, radiant, flute-playing
God who drove him.

*

My uncle (so-called *little prince*)
dropped a brass jug
on his head;

inside his shoe,
my father (so-called *littler prince*) once met a scorpion;

four floors up, he leapt
off the rain gutter, across an open alley, landing on the neighbor's roof.

None of this killed him.

He wasn't an American.
He wasn't even an Indian yet.

And not the clot, years later, though he lay on the floor, calling, though
he can't remember

what words, in which language.

*

We know of Arjuna's long talk with God,

the charioteer,

the moment:

Detach! Detach! Detach!
Birds wheeled above the battle-field.

The Song of the Lord, the work
is called:

and you must sing it.

*

Shah Jahan, of Taj
eternal love and building fame,
was locked up by his son,
who, after doing in his brother, assumed the throne and ran
the Empire five generations had amassed
into the ground. Some say
the son allowed the father
to retain his large and well-known
harem, but my father never told me

that. The story he loved best
concerned the cook of Shah Jahan:

Told he could make only one dish
for his deposed, imprisoned master,
he chose that lowly lentil staple of the poor,
Dal, because

it can be made a thousand
different ways, all richness
in variety.

*

On my father's first day in America, he had to order lunch.
Sandwich, he requested, knowing all about Americans and sandwiches.
The deli man appeared more pink than white:

Turkey, ham, roast beef, pastrami, salami, tuna salad, chicken salad, cheese...

Cheese! Oh, Cheese!

my father interrupted, glad, more than glad, delighted

to seize a possibility

which wasn't recently alive and pink and also needing lunch.
What kind of cheese, the man replied, stabbing with the mustard knife?

*

Once, in a poem, I miswrote
Deli for Delhi.

*

Back then, my mother was the only
memsahib regularly driving in New Delhi.
Austin of England, the car was called. One tire
often rolled off on the roundabouts, the great gearshift was like-wise known
for independence. Once,
on Prithiraj road, she noticed

she was passing the US ambassador's house,
her speed and direction completely free
of anyone's control.

*

If you want liberation, love

the dutiful
action.

Act dutifully. Do

not love

the fruit

of action. Whatever the result,
have no attachment.

Not the fruit, not the fruit, not the fruit—

This is the song of God's chariot wheel.

*

Friend, look out across the battlefield:

fathers, grandfathers, teachers,
uncles, brothers, sons,
grandsons and friends…

How could our Prince not love
the fruit of action?

fathers, grandfathers,
friends and sons,

Who's Prince enough to need
philosophy far more than fruits

who love you back?

        *

My mother missed her beef and so
my father paid a Muslim butcher
to deliver in the dark of night, creeping up the back steps,
while the neighbors slept the sleep of beef-free innocents.

They cursed each other for deception
and its need. *Selfish! Cruel! Unbending! Vile!*
But the butcher made his midnight missions
toting hock and haunch, the shoulder bone

of duty or love?

        *

To cure the Prince
of human love, God gave our Arjuna
God's eyes,
so he could see true nature, true reality.
He saw

all creatures, animate, inanimate, divine and mortal, all

the ones he loved were
rushing toward
were dead

*

in all the billion blazing mouths
of God.

Oh, God.

When they had strolled the palaces, trailing hands in perfumed foun-
tains, imagined ankles for those ankle-bells they heard, when they had
slid their arms into a cool silk robe, sat a horse, sucked the seeds of
pomegranates, learned hymns and how to hold a bow

this rushing toward, this being dead, this moment

was

had been and is already happening.

*

The whole world living, yet already dead.
His own hand moving, yet he'd seen
it was already ash. One Arjuna
alive, to wield a bow and act, and one who knew
the actor wouldn't last beyond the scene.

Is this how our Prince transformed his heart?
How he cut and scattered all the strings
that tied him to the lives of brothers, mothers, sons

among the weeds and black earth churned
by angry hooves?

*

It wasn't Delhi I watched burning. It was another
country, nothing to do with me. Foreigners
were locked down in the hotel. I joined
the drinking on the roof-top bar:
the clink of ice, charmingly
disparaging remarks about school days,
dumb loves, back-water towns.
Sirens so far away they were a tune.
Across the street, two men had their arms around each other.
A fight, it seemed. Occasionally,
before we fell, I saw them
through an open window framed with lace.

                    *

And when it happened, when we fell,
when the building next to me
became a cloud of fire and paperwork,
the gin glass wobbled and the man
who'd sat across from me all night,
who'd bought my drinks, who'd told me
his mother's girlhood games, her towns
and what he thought
her dreams had been, pressed his face
to my neck. No wound, no blood
that I could see

or just a drop, the tiniest of drops
caught in the glass
where it bloomed and bloomed
while the debris came down
and the sound came up and I was
rocking back and forth and singing,
but I don't know what.

*

What is that moment

called? What was
impossible is possible.

A regal sum of lentils and of sandwich meats.

*

A moment
when you hold someone
who will mistake you for his mother,

a moment when the whole world's sound
shuts off and you hear your own song
pounding in your ears,

racing chariot wheels, one moment
you're surprised to see yourself—
detached, breathing—from a long way off.

I crooned. I rubbed his back.
God knows, I promised anything.

*

This is how I picture Arjuna:
long and lean and hollowed out

the way a flute is.

*

I held the hand of my life's love

up on a palace balcony. The balustrade
had sheared away, destroying courtyard flower-beds.

We'd done whatever falling we would do

in an alcove, inlayed top-to-bottom—everywhere
were vines entwined with fruit—we found

a sandstone block, completely unadorned,
too large to sit, too small to lie down flat.

We read the plaque: *Official seat
of court musicians, who were charged with playing
for the royal court. Alleged to have been built
for the brothers Pandava.*

*

The interlude was over.

Arjuna would fight

across the battlefield, God would be the charioteer.

So well-oiled were the wheels—

the driver and the Prince
no sound

as they advanced, as Arjuna
pulled back the tight string of his bow—

                    *

A hiss, a breath

held long, let go. It hummed
into the air—

into the empty alcove
with its sandstone block,
which my love and I discovered
was too small to lie on, flat—

it ricocheted like bullet shots
fired from our mouths

into carved canopies

more vines more fruits

more—

SHHHHH.

I heard them, then—

footsteps in the far-off hall
we had already wandered through;
a note that might resolve
into a laugh

of ghostly princes

or of sight-seers
who would come after us

to stand under the writhing fruit, the blank and silent block
and wonder,

Who's been here?
A queen? A son? In this strange room
what have they thought or done?

4.

Where did it happen, I asked? Which country? Ah, said Tridib.
That's the trick. It happened everywhere, wherever you wish it.
　　　　　　　　　—Amitav Ghosh, *The Shadow Lines*

BASIC GEOGRAPHY

i.
If you die in Varanasi, you go straight to heaven,
as my mother nearly did. Free

from grueling cycles of rebirth, you'll never
have to hold your daughter, crying all night,

watch her slip a ring on her finger and promise
to love another as much as she loves you,

mourn petals whipped from roses by a brisk fall wind
or the puddle curdled with oil,

sky darkened, weather turned. You will live
with Shiva and his radiant body, as he meditates

on death, desire—the long shining cloth
that was your life. High up on Mount Kailash,

you can ask the truth of anything—
but first, you must die in Varanasi,

burn your body in the ghat,
as my mother almost did, one February.

ii.
My father's mother understood
why the Christian God had sent his son.
Relying on the good behavior
of your sons: it's what an Indian would do.
But why a mighty God would have just one—
this she couldn't credit. Of course,
it ended badly: *an only child*
will always be a sorrow to his parents.

iii.
My mother's mother promised
we would reach the Holy Land
the year I turned sixteen.
County Tipperary, she meant,
a miracle of greens, site

of her mother's teen-aged annunciation,
plagues of strained engagements
and masonry accidents. When Dr. Sullivan explained
about her liver, she waved it away:
All that cheap Communion wine.

iv.
At the Mahadevi Temple,
I wanted to become the Lady,
painted with patient eyes
and skulls ruffling her throat,
shied when the priest reached
to bless my head—I swore
his beard was alive. *Little daughter,*
have no fears. His hands
were so soft on my face,

I looked away, to find a brass pot
bristling with marigolds.
He stroked ash, sandalwood paste
above my brow— *Fear nothing.*
The fate of you and yours
is written here. I bowed
beside his toes—in socks
embossed with Playboy rabbit ears.
He was laughing, but
I held my head up straight,
felt him stake the holy mark
between my eyes,
an explorer, believing
he's the first to plant his flag.

v.
Pass down the nave,
through begettings
and crusades,
cross the transept,
we stand at the central mystery:
the flesh that isn't only flesh—
eating, sleeping, dying—
flesh that wonders, feels
betrayed, must be crowned
with thorns on a dry hillside,
or—between the lettuces—be

cudgeled by a brother with a spade.
Blood and body beneath the apse—
we swallow the incarnation's
exact longitude and latitude:
flesh and geography
dissolving on your tongue.

First Families: Cain and Abel

1.   Cain

I left by train,
taking only a blade.
How long could it take
to reach my end? The first car
carried winds repeating names.
The next one swayed
with slim bodies the humiliated
were willing to exchange.
A compartment of only moans,
whose floor was stained
by untouched offerings. A carriage
coffer of dresses still smelling
of perfume. Another bearing faces
I prayed to love. Another of loves
I happily betrayed. Another
paved with eyes expecting
explanation. Carriage after carriage.
Car of the unidentified
blurred urges. A car of fists
and fingers clutching brushes,
shovels, spoons. Why
didn't I take up my knife?
Was it snow obliterating
gate and grave with flakes
I could melt on my tongue?
The poppy's head darkening
over mulch-beds of men, bull's bone
or potato skins—the indifferent

and the shocking reds crossed
like fingers? Luck appears
like grace: a crippling need
to pay attention while the train chugs on
from its origin. I fell into the day
from my mother's curses and strains.
Out of the tunnel I came, looking
at everything. The midwife had to strike
me twice before I'd call for you.

2. Abel

I don't remember everything.
Well water tasted of metal.
In the rutted yard, the dog
choked on its chain,
repeatedly. We complained.
The ceilings were low. Not one
of the kitchen counters was level.

We had no interest in our parents' history.
We were after and before.
The woman was only our mother;
her silence was the ordinary
orbit every little family roams,
inevitable and alone
as a planet. Eve was the end
of one day, the expectation
of the next. The sun dragged

its colors down, while dust in the field
rose up. We felt the twilight haze,
stinging in the nose and throat.
She sat on the front step carefully

drying her face with her sleeve.
Inside we heard our father
washing the dirt from his hands.

3. Cain (an interview)

What time of year was it?
Spring. It was all about promise: neon crocus blinking in the drainage ditch,
everything smelling sweetly of shit. Then it was crisp, September.

Who started it?
The light. It turned the hay bales into miners' pans, the runner beans to
silver fish. It left the lanky Early Girls in shadow.

Were you angry?
Not at first. There was a bird, I don't know what kind, crying and lifting its
tail in time. At first, I wasn't looking carefully enough to be angry.

Do you regret it?

Do you regret it?

Do you regret it?
Are you asking me if I regret the world?

Are you a man or a symbol?
I'm like the little towns you fly over at night. Two streets. A cross of light.

What is the greatest advance in civilization that you've witnessed?
Orthodontia.

Please answer seriously. We'd like to know how men and women today differ now from how we were at first.

I'm telling you, modern men and women have great teeth.

Fine. Vanilla or Chocolate?

Chocolate.

Innie or outie?

Outie.

Favorite color?

Blue.

Favorite word?

You.

Favorite food?

A stranger.

No, really.

O.k. The radish.

Tell us about the mark.

The question mark? Look, it's a hook. It's shaped like the back of the head, the spine wide open.

Given everything, how happy are you, on a scale of one to ten?

What a phrase: given everything.

Please answer on a scale of one to ten.

One, seven, nine, ten.

Do you think you'll ever be happy?

What makes you think I'm not?

What about joy? What about hope?
If I write lip, it hopes for sip; it gets lucky joy with hip; it's surprised by sick, ditch, stick.

What about mercy? Consolation? What about redemption in the face of history?

We'd like an answer.
I think that's in a different book.

Is there anything you'd like to add?
Stippled, whip, nipple, grip, cripple skip...

And what are we supposed to make of that?
Trip, kiss, nibble, spit.

4. Abel

Face it: the Greek god ate his children; elsewhere
one brother milled a cousin with his carriage wheel;
last week, in Coeur D'Alene, a women tried to drown
her children in an infant's tub—

I won't say I knew exactly what would happen,
but when the fire under our offerings laughed
and caused wheat kernels, bones, stalks
to crack and pop, we listened.
When we let the lamb's blood run
over the tabernacle steps,
it erased my dusty footprints.

MY BROTHER'S KEEPER

On July 13, 2002, unidentified militants attacked the Qasim
Nagar slum near Jammu, in Indian Kashmir, killing 27. The
militants arrived dressed as sadhus (Hindu holy men), carrying
automatic weapons and grenades in bags and among the folds of
their robes.

Details kill me too.
What's one pock-faced dead boy?
Who counts the dullest crime?
Why should it matter
the men with guns pretended
to be sadhus? When it comes
it's all the same in holy robes,
creased khakis or brocades.
What if they hadn't all been huddled
on the bania's floor for a cricket match,
blow by blow, on All India Radio:
the batter's whites, the hoarse crowd's roar,
the headman's cheek inking a record
of love on his neighbor's sari blouse,
spattered sheet dumped down a well?
If I describe the line the dead boy drew
on the dirt floor of his home,
learning his letters with the sharp tine
of a chicken bone—Now you see,
it's dirty work to make it shine.
How smooth the stone he carried
in his pocket? Round ones kept
under his bed, with plastic soldiers
and gum wrappers. You have to know
you can't trust me. I save everything I see—

the cat carting away a thumb
into a bank of rose bushes,
and from the chinar tree
the crows are dropping bobby-pins.

Love Song
(Orion's Belt: The King Brothers'
Murder Trial, Florida, 2002)

Dark, maybe already fallen, for all
the star looks fixed. The light I see
from my backyard, a mark for time

it takes to cross cold space.
That I don't trip in the bedroom
before I reach the switch, that's memory,

a burning stick that lights the ditch between
myself and what I've done. I'm certain
of the desk's waist-high wood lip,

where my belt is hung and every use
to which they've both been put:
hand-me-downs they've stored or cinched

or when I bent above the one
the other cracked the arc that linked
me with my father's grip. Belt and desk

are discipline and thrift. To know
the size, the weight, the purpose of a thing—
it's not enough that I and it exist. Every object

must be struck with an illuminating force;
what I know of it is what's reflected back.
In firelight the buckle of belt gleams red,

sunlight shows it pale with all its nicks,
if I sit, the strap-length grows as though it fit
someone of twice my width. Distance

from ourselves to what we want to know
is sometimes circumstance. Lay the leather
on the desk, measure and be done

with understanding it. Principle
gives inches—twenty-six—and four
round holes in brown and gold.

Among pens and envelopes, I've kept this:
newsprint—above the fold a picture
of the fat end of a baseball bat. What's known

spelled out below in black and white—
the father's body found reclining in an easy-chair,
the sons' complete confessions—will not explain

what happened in that house. They are and are not
boys. The bat, another thing that is and never is
itself entirely. All the light we cast,

flares and sparks, consumes, reveals in parts.
You, who hold the trick, hang silent in the dark,
although we act, like strap and buckle, glint.

LOVE SONG (SURAT, GUJARAT, 1992)

In December of 1992, Surat was the site of the most explosive and
brutal Hindu-Muslim communal riots since Partition.

From the bedroom they moved to the street.
Just as all the afternoons they'd spoiled
her with balloons, soda pops, bright plastic rings,
there was laughter. After, they set her petticoat alight.

Could've been me, daughter of darkest things—
balloons, soda pop, plastic rings—
They split the whole of her from life.
You're shocked: they were her neighbors and they'd watched

her running circles in the new red top
her mother made, for joy of having limbs
that spin the noisy rosy town around,
fed her sugared almonds from their palms,

said they loved her. And they did. You think
they undid their love or proved they never did
by what they've done. Here's the whole horror—
pink balloons twirling away into the sun.

Think of all the other words you know
love by: mother, god, citizen. Which one
is nothing more than what you'd choose?
You've answered every one with, *why.*

For I did love my neighbor. Do.
Balloons. Fistfuls of silver rings.
Shiny loves are children's things.
You'll say I've made love meaningless,

that I'm trying to excuse, that I don't see
the girl without her legs below the knee.
I'm only arguing what we can use
of love is not the half of it. You're sure

you are a true neighbor. That you couldn't,
wouldn't. But to know the whole of you—
my lover of soda pop, heart-shaped balloons—
I need the other names for what you do.

AT THE TIKI LOUNGE

You've got a pretty face, he said.
I thought he meant I seemed likely

To listen. Thought he might explain
The way he lost his lines and leg.

Instead, he's on to market day in Basra. Sweet
Apples there the size of knuckles. Curtains

Made of Chinese lace for sheiks' car windows.
Then, this old guy asks us in, he says:

The granddaughter serving up behind his shop.
It was disgusting. Hot stringy meat, some gritty

Sauce. Worse even than our Army shit.
But you don't piss the locals off.

Hearts and minds, you know.
And hospitality's the bitch out there.

So we keep eating. The granddaughter's just piling
Servings on. You have the look of them, he says,

I mean, you look a bit like her. Our drinks are up.
I'm free to pay and go. I don't have anything to say to this.

Then, the old guy—shit—the old guy starts in laughing. I sit
To hear the end. I don't know what I owe or whom I owe it to.

He's busting up. We don't know what the fuck to do.
It might be camel balls or some real toxic shit.

Lt. keeps asking, but the bastard won't shut up.
Everyone gets nervous. Everyone starts shifting around.

I thought J.B. was maybe gonna pop him one. Then,
The girl just throws the spoon. She hits Lt. and runs.

Here, he leans toward me, gently pinning my wrist.
Next day, one of our guys is sick.

Some FNG starts joking that the old guy fed us
Parts of kidnapped journalists. That made J.B. get mad.

He pauses as he pays the bartender for both our drinks.
And then, he says, *the CO showed and broke it up.*

I let my breath out in a rush. Turn my hand so it's palm up.
So nothing happened? Nothing really happened that day?

I feel his forearm tense, tendons tightening fingers and wrist.
I'm telling you what happened, he says, pushing my hand away.

NOBODY NATION

(West)

Out of the ribbons of heat, trumpets blaring, lights flashing rapturously, the state trooper directs us to the side of the Arizona highway, begins yelling at my father in Spanish. Red dust and sage-bush and I know, instinctively, this isn't something I'm allowed to see, try to train my eyes on saguaros. Earlier, as we'd wheeled down black tarmac, they'd stood like cartoon families, row after row of small gray sisters, large mothers of green, arms raised: *Come out with your hands up!*, a cactus game, where little ones and big surrender over and over. I keep expecting my father will open his mouth and in spiked, precise English quote Locke on rights accruing naturally. Instead, when I gather the courage to peek, he is inclining his earth-hewn head, as the man shouts, *COMPRENDO* and I realize this is another language he's always known.

(East)

In Nizamuddin marketplace, my mother ponders piles of pale towels, a housewarming gift, as the man behind the counter flashes paan-pinked teeth and assures her, *Finest quality, Madame, 300 rupees.* With a careful look at me, he says in Hindi, *Tell your Memsahib it's a good price and we'll split the overcharge, you and me, 50-50, like brother and sister.* My mother smiles beatifically, her eyes tree-green, by which she means for me to play along, keeping her Hindi secret. We're perfect in our parts, me the secret, she the memsahib to the hilt, ordering fleets of wiry attendants up ladders and down to the bottom of storage bins, sailing out with a package wrapped in string. In the street, I see her face is set like a plain white plate. But she motions to a shop where I always beg for rosewater ice cream. I hand her the brother-money and under a sign where a rosy milkmaid dances for her blue-skinned lover, we spend our gains on sweets.

(South)

I show my father a page from my eighth-grade history textbook:

Although the South was well known for its anti-miscegenation policies, most states had similar laws.

STATE	FIRST LAW PASSED	LAW REPEALED	RACES BANNED FROM MARRYING WHITES	NOTE
Arizona	1865	1962	Blacks, Asians, Filipinos, Indians	Filipinos ("Malays") and Indians ("Hindus") added to list of "races" in 1931
California	1850	1948	Blacks, Asians, Filipinos	
Colorado	1864	1957	Blacks	
Idaho	1864	1959	Blacks, Native Americans, Asians	
Indiana	1818	1965	Blacks	
Maryland	1692	1967	Blacks, Filipinos	
Montana	1909	1953	Blacks, Asians	
Nebraska	1855	1963	Blacks, Asians	
Nevada	1861	1959	Blacks, Native Americans, Asians, Filipinos	
North Dakota	1909	1955	Blacks	
Oregon	1862	1951	Blacks, Native Americans, Asians, Native Hawaiians	
South Dakota	1909	1957	Blacks, Asians, Filipinos	
Utah	1852	1963	Blacks, Asians, Filipinos	
Wyoming	1913	1965	Blacks, Asians, Filipinos	

My father considers the page, hums a little, tunelessly, then lashes his newspapers back into place—creaseless, tall and straight. On the black and white columns, figures seem to twist and fly. At first, I think it's Urdu script, but when I refocus my eyes, I'm facing the messages of *The New York Times*.

(North)

It's the wife who shows me how to top and tail French green beans, placing
the knife at a forty-five degree angle, so the slender bodies taper, *Artfully*,
she says. Her husband watches election season commentary on the kitchen
TV. They are throwing a dinner party; I am earning my books and cigarettes
and everything feels bright under recessed halogens. During commercial
break, the husband casually, *So, tell me, are you a citizen?* The beans are
stacked neatly on a chilled glass tray and I wonder if he means *Can you vote?*
or *Will I pay you under the table?* The guests drift in. I blanche and plate
and scrub their tile clean. It isn't until I'm enjoying the Volvo's heated seats,
watching the snow-banks streaked with road debris that he puts his hand
on my knee. The moon dips low, I'm only a few minutes from home and I
know.

(Pacific)

When my father becomes a citizen, they re-take his fingerprints, repeatedly. Outside, there are coconut trees and the sun is headed for the sea. *I'm sorry, sir,* says the officer, good-naturedly, *You're a man of mystery! All the identifying whorls have worn away.* They're forced to press his palms to their forms. As we leave, traveling a long hall lined with portraits of past presidents, my father whispers to me, *I kept the good lines for myself.*

Fire, House, Me

Bless the last breath left
    In the perfume vial.

Bless the dialect
    In which the ficus confessed, stripping herself of leaves.

Bless whatever the faucet believed
    To sing as though there were no end

To singing, before turning off. Bless the years
    Washed down the drain.

Bless teacups, bless beds, bless the locked birdcage,
    Bless words that stained linoleum,

And the parade of plate and tine and blade—
    They flashed. They cut and fed.

The roof is gone, the windows, half the frame. Bless
    The table's metal legs and the upright remains

Of what I am: two scorched posts
    Of happiness, a lintel beam of shame.

I have no tears, no salt, no rage—
    Bless the ruined house, bless our temple,

All its secret chambers forever
    Exposed to heaven.

YOU GIVE ME FEVER

Slowly, ceiling fans wheel over me,
The air on my face, a hand
With roughened fingertips. It doesn't hurt

To be made of other's sadnesses. Your own
Will be kept company. This, I say
To the doctor wearing a pained smile

And soup stains on his pressed, white shirt,
Then avert my eyes. I can't stand straight
But I'm still mannerly. I can wait

For the quarrel on the telephone wires to be resolved:
That abacus of birds endlessly recalculates
What is added and taken from the sum of us—

Fate contained in the smallest bodies.
There is no medicine for this. The fire has to burn
My imperfections out, the soup-stained doctor says.

My mother's voice is like milk in the drain;
The sheets are stiff with bleach and river dust.
I am a citizen of beds and heat.

For once, I have no need to say, *Yes.*
I can carry it: rags and broth bowls are borne away.
For once, I don't have to keep

My eyes open and I am not hungry.

ARRIVING, NEW DELHI

Smoke. Ocher smolders. Blue
sparks. Below the airplane's
steady arcs, the neon lights are

embers. Over the city's central rings
a flash, the tipping silver
wings. Over discotheques, the temple
dancers' ankle bells. Boys
selling oranges, cool feet
in public fountains. Great cows lounge
on garbage heaps. The steep dome
of the Friday Mosque. Burger and marble
Moghul palaces. Then,

tires slamming down on pitch.
Heat, a furnace in the ears.
Doors open and the blood pounds out
its local language along every limb.
Smell ashes. Men. Jasmine
climbing on a fence. A taxi driver
turbaned in a tongue of flame
says, *Sister, I can take you into the city.*
Sister, shall I take you home?

FROM THE AFTERLIFE

I wanted to be a bone—white like
the Taj Mahal, hard as a puritan—

when vein and wish are stripped,
still able to rattle the essential notes.

But no music gets made when you pit
your self against ideas of yourself.

Dust suits me better. Grey-brown fleck—
I can mix, move into the smallest space,

spark the grittiest tunes. Divide me
into fifty states: winsome, wondering, crazed, my face

scattered by teaspoon. Over the Great Basin
of played out mines and salts rising in a haze,

over hard farmed heartland, the bent
fair-headed wheat, the combine's cloud,

silt along the fat lip of river bed. Semis
hissing and grumbling in tongues.

I can still feel the hum of the telephone wires,
running from one life to another. I filled the lines

in case a story is a body, in case we lose our place.
Hello? Friend? I can touch everything,

but can't stop thinking. Turns out, thoughts
granulate. Turns out, I never was a girl, I was all

those girls, a girl statue, torch raised, you know the one—
standing in the harbor, wearing a sari.

The tide foams up. Now, I'm so much dust,
I am a continent, absorbing—a thimble full

of mother, angry powder, laughing specks, froth,
filth, lover, crying cinders, particles of mineral wind.

I'm proof that nothing is lost.
You can breathe me in.

FOR THE SURVIVORS

Begin with a seed. Begin with the father and the mother, your first Adam and Eve. Begin with what falls from the tree: you can live on bruised and sweet. Begin with a monsoon breeze, begin with a flood, begin with miles of silk and mud and the wings of cranes and the stilt-like legs of a house with no one left inside. Begin with a young wife burying her sons and books riding the tide until they're caught and their philosophies dried out on laundry lines. Begin with a pen, begin with a cage. Begin with the memory of what they said while you tried to turn your face away. Begin with bargains, with stains, the names of towns built over towns built over graves, begin with your life burned down. Begin with the god who hasn't been seen since the burning bush or the goddess who steps into the flames like a housewife into a dress, or a fairy tale of hair so long that love climbed up—begin by putting your mouth to the mouth of your dreams. Begin with midnight rain and wild reeds, begin with hair and tendons, teeth. Begin with what never goes away: a highway pricked by gravel and stars, low beams on wind and trucks and emptiness. Begin. It starts with being, ends like a ringing bell: Begin. Begin. Ring your self.

Notes

1. *My Father's Hopscotch, 1942*: In August of 1942, the All India Congress Committee adopted the "Quit India Resolution," calling for complete independence from Britain. The British government responded by incarcerating all of the committee leaders, including Mohandas K. Gandhi. Strikes swept the country as over 100,000 were arrested. Rana Bhai literally means "Brother Rana," but does not indicate a blood relative. In South Asia, it is common to refer to non-family members by familial titles as a way of showing affection and respect. Naana means maternal grandfather. Begums are Muslim ladies of social rank. Jaggery is traditional, unprocessed sugar.

2. *He Who Does Not Have the Church As His Mother Does Not Have God As His Father:* a phrase attributed to Augustine of Hippo.

3. *Polaroid City:* The spring of 1947 marked the beginning of the violence that would accompany India's independence and its partition into two nations. In *The Other Side of Silence: Voices from the Partition of India*, Urvashi Butalia writes:

> The political partition of India caused one of the great human convulsions of history. Never before or since have so many people exchanged their homes and countries so quickly. In the space of a few months, over twelve million people moved between the new, truncated India and the two wings, East and West, of the newly created Pakistan…Slaughter sometimes accompanied and sometimes prompted their movement…Estimates of the dead vary from 200,000 (a contemporary British figure) to two million (a later Indian estimate), but that somewhere well above one million people died is now widely accepted. As always there was widespread sexual savagery: about 75,000 women are thought to have been abducted and raped by men of religions different than their own (and indeed

sometimes by men of their own religion). Thousands of families were divided, homes were destroyed, crops left to rot, villages abandoned. (*The Other Side of Silence: Voices from the Partition of India,* Urvashi Butalia (New Delhi: Penguin Books, 1998), 3).

A month earlier, on February 21, 1947, Polaroid's Edwin Land unveiled the first instant camera, capable of transforming any image into a finished photograph in 60 seconds.

4. *Visiting Indira Gandhi's Palmist*: Indira Gandhi was assassinated by two of her bodyguards in 1984. She was shot with 31 rounds, 30 of which found their mark.

5. *Light*: It is estimated that somewhere between 75,000 and 100,000 women were abducted during Partition. In September of 1947, both the Indian and Pakistani governments agreed to attempt to "recover" abducted persons and reunite them with their original families. India's official Abducted Persons (Restoration and Recovery) Act was signed in 1949. Some scholars estimate that 10% of abducted women were located through this program. The program, however, was fraught with problems. Sexual violence, forced marriages and the resulting birth of children complicated both laws and loyalties. In some cases, the women's original families would not accept them back. In other cases, women didn't want to return to their original families, but their wishes were not taken into account and many were forcibly repatriated.

6. *Havan, 1921*: In the early 1920's, Gandhi began advocating the destruction of British cloth as part of his non-cooperation movement. A *havan* is a common Hindu ceremony of purification, performed for occasions ranging from housewarmings to funerals. Offerings, like rice, milk, wood and flowers are placed into a ritual fire, which carries offerings and prayers to the Gods.

7. *Love Song (Surat, Gujarat, 1992)*: Arson, looting and violence began after the destruction of the Babri Mosque by Hindu nationalists. The event sparked other riots across the nation.

8. *Love Song* (*Orion's Belt: The King Brothers' Murder Trial, Florida, 2002*): The newspaper photograph refers to the 2002 trial of brothers Derek and Alex King, who were accused of killing their father with a baseball bat.

9. *Nobody Nation*: The title was inspired by Derek Walcott's line, "either I'm nobody or I'm a nation," from the poem "*Schooner Flight.*"

TITLES FROM ELIXIR PRESS

POETRY

Circassian Girl by Michelle Mitchell-Foust

Imago Mundi by Michelle Mitchell-Foust

Distance From Birth by Tracy Philpot

Original White Animals by Tracy Philpot

Flow Blue by Sarah Kennedy

A Witch's Dictionary by Sarah Kennedy

The Gold Thread by Sarah Kennedy

Monster Zero by Jay Snodgrass

Drag by Duriel E. Harris

Running the Voodoo Down by Jim McGarrah

Assignation at Vanishing Point by Jane Satterfield

Her Familiars by Jane Satterfield

The Jewish Fake Book by Sima Rabinowitz

Recital by Samn Stockwell

Murder Ballads by Jake Adam York

Floating Girl (Angel of War) by Robert Randolph

Puritan Spectacle by Robert Strong

Keeping the Tigers Behind Us by Glenn J. Freeman

Bonneville by Jenny Mueller

Cities of Flesh and the Dead by Diann Blakely

The Halo Rule by Teresa Leo

Perpetual Care by Katie Cappello

The Raindrop's Gospel: The Trials of St. Jerome and St. Paula by Maurya Simon

Prelude to Air from Water by Sandy Florian

Let Me Open You A Swan by Deborah Bogen

Cargo by Kristin Kelly

Spit by Esther Lee

Rag & Bone by Kathrym Nuernberger

Kingdom of Throat-stuck Luck by George Kalamaras

Mormon Boy by S. Brady Tucker

Nostalgia for the Criminal Past by Kathleen Winter

Little Oblivion by Susan Allspaw

Quelled Communiqués by Chloe Joan Lopez

Stupor by David Ray Vance

Curio by John Nieves

The Rub by Ariana-Sophia Kartsonis

Visiting Indira Gandhi's Palmist by Kirun Kapur

FICTION

How Things Break by Kerala Goodkin

Nine Ten Again by Phil Condon

Memory Sickness by Phong Nguyen

Troglodyte by Tracy DeBrincat

LIMITED EDITION CHAPBOOKS

Juju by Judy Moffat

Grass by Sean Aden Lovelace

X-testaments by Karen Zealand

Rapture by Sarah Kennedy

Green Ink Wings by Sherre Myers

Orange Reminds You Of Listening by Kristin Abraham

In What I Have Done & What I Have Failed To Do by Joseph P. Wood

Hymn of Ash by George Looney

Bray by Paul Gibbons